Hackles

Editing: Kelsey Sipple
Cover design: Angelicque Roa
Cover art: *Arctic Hare*, 1841, John James Audubon

ISBN 9798991853002 (paperback)
ISBN 9798991853019 (ebook)

First Edition
Published by Girl Noise Press
girlnoise.press

"What do you want — a cliff over a city?
A foreland, sloped to sea and overgrown with roses?
These people live here."

MURIEL RUKEYSER, THE BOOK OF THE DEAD

Hackles

poems by
Makayla Danielle Gay

GIRL NOISE

Contents

Watching Season

I am watching   (being watched I'm told)
My neighbor across the courtyard flicks on his kitchen light to
home himself.
He turns on his air fryer and immediately takes off his clothes.
(he watches me)   (eat the skin of an apple off the blade)

I watch Jesse move like a minute across our apartment.
He has stopped going outside. Even to smoke.
He bends his head over the gas range to light his cigarettes.
I say that the air is stale and he nails the window shut.

(I am)   (being watched)
   he says, binoculars uncapped.
Jesse used to love birding.
In Miami,
          he favored the swamps and their blue herons.
I liked walking the beaches' stiff quiet, dark for all the turtles to
bash their little skulls through shells.
The hotel rooms were stacked up like fish bowls, lit up with each
person living a life.
I had never felt so loved as I had when I came out of the ocean
& felt him watching me. Eyes passing me back and forth like
(slip)   (ping clay.)

Jesse has taken to newspapering over the windows.
He keeps his ears pressed to monitor the spore molds
of conversation
inside the drywall.
(We are no longer)   just   (being watched)

My granny used to get us to bed or to sweep under the rug
telling us
(God is watching)   (God is watching)

I wake up to thrashing in the living room.
Our dog doesn't bark, he flips to his cooler side.
Jesse is out there kneeling. Yelling weeping begging.
He said that They have all gotten in.
I kneel and show him how to touch the warped flooring,
the crumb-filled stubble of the cowhide rug.
The things that are here. The lamp is left on all night. It does not
flicker.
(   )   (   )

I don't go back into the ocean, I swim into the sea.
While swimming in the breaks, a man watches me from the shore.
I dive in and out to feel myself pass back and forth
through his gaze. He invites me sailing.
He points to his chipped rudder and tells me how he and his son
were attacked by orcas last year near Spain. He says that it's
because there's not enough fish anymore. The watching boats chum
up the waters to draw them out. *Driving them like crazy,* he said. The
orcas had bumped beneath their sailboat, thrashed the water, and
tasted the engine. The son threw carrots to try to lure them away.
The father began beating their beaks with oars.

The boat took on water. He prepared the life raft.
All at once the orcas swam away
leaving empty carrots murmuring in the water.

We're going
on up
the hill

Singing with
the hill

Sleeping in
the hill

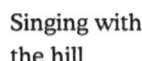

Today, another girl from the mountains died.

Although I heard about it from the paper —
she was pretty, after all, with an orthodontist-laid smile
french tips glistening moons, eyes blue, the grass
in her father's yard was so green...
I am not sad. I am not thinking about her.

I am thinking about the gas left in my car. The voicemail from my
sister. If this winter will be bad. If I'll get paid on time. The long
black hairs I keep pulling from the back of my throat.
The chicken defrosting on the counter.

I wish that I could say that when I find these long black hairs,
I picture the girl in the back row of our remedial geometry class
and think *it should have been me,*
but I don't.
> When I close my eyes tonight
> instead of turning around to look
> into her face as she sat,
> twirling the ends of her hair across her upper lip —

I just fall asleep.

Cow Pond Haibun

Snake found on cow pond island. Hoed open; infants wormed out. We practiced cruelty so often, it felt like a mistake. A copperhead bit the neighbor woman when she was pregnant with her third. She popped its maw from her ankle bone like a nerf bullet. *That's why that child stays so mean,* folks would say. Oh, for a reason to be wicked too! We'd ground each other into red earth, press june bugs into ears — then in kindness fresh as potato bulbs — take the june bugs out. Us — loose in the fields and hills, banshee-wild, but on Sundays we minded good — stalk still in our slick-shined shoes. Some weeknights too — when the deacons pitched the tent, sweat blooming on their backs, God's voice so big it might knock down walls. We practiced being filled, writhing between leather musks of tobacco. Listening for the tongues that would set down on us, licking in fire behind the ears like the deer on salt blocks so we could speak the language of the angels, Gabriel and all of them in their tide-white dresses. Waiting the voice of God, we saw the monk work of the field: the cicadas singing under the bent boughs singing their bug hymns, a garden snake slippy spun through. The snakes we found out by the pond looked so different than the snakes brought in glass boxes during the pitch-sway of God calling. We would like to answer too;

to be delivered from anything. A mark to say that no matter
the tiny evils — we are better; we are loved. We hoped the
snakes would be set out behind the tent to scythe through
the grass between car tires clicking cold to tell their friends
that they were shook by the Great Big Hands and had been
delivered too

Fine things of the grass,
God knows us clear — serpents sing
ing out: bless us

             s

                    s

                      .

We approached death with full plates.
Once the cicadas fell
from their slick resin
we drove Chevrolets full
up to the hill.

Us kids squatted out of sight
to pluck legs off daddy longs
till the preaching and tinny singing
stopped, and we answered by
tearing free, screaming — wild
like banshees, like the ones our
family left back on a further hill.

I've never used to think of death and dying.
I only thought of biscuits still warm
in their tin and smiling in pretty
dresses next to cousins who didn't
have to climb up the hill this year.

Learning to Drive a Stick

Dad never taught me how to drive a stick,
and too many times I had stripped the gears
off my brothers' trucks when they had an afternoon of patience.
My grandad, too, used to flood the clutch —
and by that I mean, he drove his Ford Pinto into the neighbor's
pond.
The sheriff decided to stop letting him drive drunk after that.
In the hospital, the detective asked in curt English
why I didn't leave after someone
slammed me into a concrete hedge
using the fist of a rented Skoda.

I thought,
I don't know why I'm with my boyfriend either —
the muscle of my *no* had atrophied,
as it had in Granny's legs back in Kentucky.
Drinking and smashed fenders
has the same nose for my family as high cholesterol.
In the night after,
I did what the lady with the stale perfume at those Al Anon meet-
ings said,
let him tread through his own decisions
but who would choose to stand on the shore and

watch arms cut through dark empty waters?

He tried to climb the fire escape drunk after I locked up the soft,
empty dark of my apartment to keep him from
re-emerging, dripping wet in my bed.
He slipped.
That's how I knew he was there,
his nails made a *tschk* sound as he dug into the metal ladder,
boots grazing back over the grating of the footholds.
I carried him down from the landing where he puddled.
Do not ask me how I carried a man down a fire escape.
Granny said I was always too skinny — weak
she meant, never ate enough, but she oversalted
everything: biscuits, beans, coffee —
Dad told me she poured in the salt to cut Grandad's hangovers.
She thought she could dry up the slug in him.

He used to hit her — not *him*, not *me*.
Grandad used to hit Granny.
Not just with his fists that's why,
even after he's been dead for longer than
I've been alive, we eat supper off plastic plates.

After I drug him into the safety of the elevator,
I hit him. Not him, *him*.
In the morning he doesn't remember, but God I wish he did —
I wish he knew what the meat of my fists tasted like,
what it felt like to be mashed into the size of my palm,
so he could know what it's like to be a passenger.

I slept in the bathroom so I could lock the door.
I heard him in my little bed.
I could hear him piss in my little bed.
I heard him roll over, fall off my little bed, groan, gurgle —
then heard nothing at all.

I wish I could hit him. Not *him* — Grandad.
I wish I was alive when they dredged up his Ford Pinto,

the stocked catfish still flopping in the chapped leather of the
backseats.
If I was the one to have found him, I'd have drug him
to the grass bank and whaled on him
till I'd killed that part that would've born me
so I'd never have to learn to drive a stick,
never have to fail at driving a stick,
never have to be stuck, flooding the engine, mashing
the clutch, shifting from first to third and lurching back instead.
If I never had to learn how to drive a stick, I'd never have to
hate someone so much that I would lay on the cool gloss of the tile
and think about what would happen if I stayed in the bathroom,
closed
my eyes while he — who I promised my forever,
would drown in a teacup's worth of sick.

Two of the paramedics that carried him out, nodded down to him,
He looks like the Marlboro Man.
Was that why I stayed?
Another paramedic hung back to speak in the stairwell,
It's not your fault.
Would Granny have wanted to kiss her like I had?
or would she have stared back blankly, finished scraping
congealed beans from plastic plates as if she'd
never considered such a thing in her life...

Swamp Molly

I sat with a boy by the lake
who put his hand on my knee to tell me what
the JV soccer team knew
about Swamp Molly,
a tangled mass of every thing/one found at the bottom of the lake
who drifts from cove to cove, shrieking.

I got up
        not because I knew fear predicted sex
        but to try to see something that moved around in its own
        hunger.

She lives in the lake
the TVA made
so we all had lights to flick off
then back on after the Lord's prayer

& to power the blue orb glow of a Gamecube
reflecting into the whites of my brothers' eyeballs
as they sat, down the hall, in such a tight line
I see one profiled slope of Brother.

I have a fourth, somewhere

in Mississippi felling trees.
He had a hole in his timber boots, so small
a brown recluse got in.
By the time he lurched out of the woods
        his foot was graying from his body.
I was so afraid of what I might let in
I slept with my sneakers on.

What I am really afraid of,
               I tell my friend
once we are all 30 and know better,
is going through the glass tunnels
on those slowly moving walkways in an aquarium
and looking up and seeing —
              a crack?
no, no.
        Seeing nothing
        being at the bottom of emptiness.

The last time I saw myself from across the lake —
        I swam
            losing everything around me.

I've sat still, hunched
my nails like
animal deep ragged moons.
I used to follow instructions like
        c'mere baby
            come —
I've been called sweet enough times
        and more than that
when I've had someone else's fingers in my mouth
I think of carrots —
           ^

I am moving my hunger back towards myself.
I want to tell this boy what I know about fear;
I am the tunnel to kiss on the mouth, my own collection of

sweet
sink
        rot.

Horse Facts

//   Horses in the Rapture

In the 8th grade, our class went to a horse auction
and a man in a suit & cowboy hat taught us that
the slightest movement
could be interpreted as a "bid."
I've been paralyzed since,
thinking that my body could be misunderstood enough
to be stuck with a half-ton stallion that could kick
collapse my lungs
or split my head like a rock melon.
I miss the point all the time —
at least in basketball, I could get a H O R S E
my brothers would let me play until H O R S E S
sometimes till H O R S E S-I N-T H E-P A S T U R E.

Cousin Keisha kept an old Amish buggy horse named Fiesta
in a fallow part of our farm.
It was 18- hands tall and had never seen tail lights and belt buckles.
When they first tried to bring Fiesta home, he wouldn't step into
the hitch haul.
Uncle Wendell drove to the next county over to
buy two cases of Bud
so Fiesta could be stumble-sway-pushed inside.

My friend had a horse named Susie Q.
who wasn't brought in from the pasture in time.
They all made it inside the house and watched from
the basement window
as the tornado plucked up Susie Q.
and placed her down yards further.
Imagine, not knowing about weather systems or gravity.
Susie Q. must have had to accept the fact
that this is a thing that can happen from time to time
since she couldn't fully arch her neck back
to check the sky for other floating horses.

Susie Q. & I are alike in the way
that we are both worried about the Rapture.
I am afraid that one day I will come home
to an empty house with all the lights on
Jesus will have taken everyone out to buy cigarettes and I will be
left —
shifting foot to foot, alone
save for all the horses.
& we will have to make small talk somehow.

Untitled With Voice Memos

Memo 1: Oxford Crest Apartments, Seattle

In September,
I woke up to my boyfriend sitting on a kitchen chair
dragged over to our bed.
A knife sat, an open wound, on his thigh.
He handed me a mug of coffee, told me not to worry.
The reason he held a knife to my throat as I slept
was to get the voices living between the floorboards
to scream so loud I could hear them too.

He made me listen to the 52 minutes of emptiness
gathered as proof of the conversations blooming
in our apartment walls. When I listened,
I heard the simmer of traffic on the street below
Oh, I prayed to see a figure emerge from the voice memo's
flat lines.
I asked God for a mountain range of broken canine teeth
plotting to kill him, and rape me.

When he came to me
bearing the frosted curve of the entryway light cover

filled brown with a salad of dead ladybugs
I said,
I guess you were right all along.
The whole apartment is bugged.
He laid his face in my lap and cried.

Memo 2: What They Said

If you hold that knife, she will split open to all the work we have done to undo.

When you fall asleep she slips out to slick herself in the oil of loose men.She fucks
them all. 8 altogether. On the upstairs deck, she,split wide open, her moans sounded like

^h/

^h /

^h/

^h/

^h /

Hold that knife and she will make the same sounds and tell you everything. We've been watching ██████████████. She has been here too, watching from our place within ███ █████. She is disappointed in you she is marrying you as a joke remember that month you couldn't get hard? she has told everyone about that. when you left the diagrams of the genius novel on your desk, she awoke after to erase it all she undid it so you woke every mornin to a hard, blank page after a night of brilliance we've been working to undo because you know the secret.The Secret. The █████. The █████ . She knows the secret too. This is your chance to get back the secret. She keeps it in the divot of her throat between her collar bones. She is not even asleep. She will scream when you hold the knife and we will come and stop you to save the secret.

She is waking.
She knows.

Memo 3: Lunch With My Therapist

When I FaceTimed Dr. Lewis
she was eating lunch.
I told her about the voices,
the hidden Gatorade bottles of piss,
the crystal meth & the stolen license plates.
She nodded
rubbing the sticker off her peach,
"It's no joke," she said
and plunged her thumbs into the throat.
"Some people bounce back
after a few dry weeks.
With some, it's a box
that can never be closed."
With a suck pull,
she showed me the inside of the halves.
The pit.

"It's been opened."

Memo 4: Bridal Shoppe Conversations

I smooth out the creases
in the satin-lined crepe with the hooked mouth
of a steamer.
I help a woman into a gown in the dim dressing room.
We do not want them to see themselves in private.
We want to be in private with them
to tell them what they see.

She jumps a bit when my fingertips brush her lower back
as I tug and lace.
Embarrassed, I ask about her fiancé so she will forget my cold
hands.
They met on an app, or in high school, or at a tech firm.
She forgets about my cold. I have not slept in days.
She asks me how long I have been engaged.
The ring is caught in a crook of lace net
in the woman's underwear.
Oh, I told her, it's been going on a while now.

Memo 5: When They Became Quiet

They didn't.
It was like I left a party crowded with strangers.
    Leaving the house, I heard the din skidding the sidewalk
    behind me, the windows still dark-lit, shapes flickering between
each gust of light from a freshly lit cigarette. When I grabbed my
jacket by the door the conversation didn't pause to let me pass
through.

    It is a party I will never turn back to.
    Even as I left, I never considered an "after."

I will stop thinking about the party now.

Memo 6: Sections of Undoing

There is so much lost when the mind goes,
and it's not even about the mind:
- Party invitations
- The trust in an open window and its breeze
- Hospitable silences
- Camera phones
- Sleep
- Boutonnières of venus fly traps
- Rent deposits
- A honeymoon in Patagonia

When it all began he was 37. Then he turned 38.
I hope he is 39 now. I hope he will be 40.

Basil

Have I told you how badly I wanted to lift the shroud of
Saint Basil of Ostrog
to see if the smell of basil lingered in his bones?

I didn't —

        not because I'm scared of the dead or the sacred
or to discover that miracles no longer exist

        but because of this huge gray priest
that stood there with these eyes as sad as milk saucers.

He gave me the tiniest nod when I approached the body
and taught me how to make the sign of the cross.

I felt like I had been given a whole crate of oranges.

Kick the Blocks
For Glacier Girl

This one summer Pa worked at getting his pilot's license. Twice a week he'd go fly with a man named Bea Arthur who lived down the street and kept a jumpy two-seater. They'd take off from the field behind the elementary school. Bea would set the engine and Pa would kick the blocks. Once, Bea turned to Pa mid-air to show him a fistful of bolts he kept in his vest pocket, "I hope these weren't meant to be important."

Bea salvaged the seats from *Glacier Girl,* a Lockheed shot down over Greenland in World War II. *Where did Bea get those seats,* we wanted to know. "He dug them from the ice." We'd sit in the yard waiting for them to path over the house so we could wave. Pa would insist that he waved back. After supper, he'd log his flight time so the hours of watching could count towards knowing. We'd ask him to describe the roof of our house, what the neighbors up the hill were doing in their yard, and if there really was a pool on top of the I-75 McDonald's.
    Flying is uncovering the earth

                              from ground and shape.
Some nights we could hear the high school football game from across town; time and sound stayed bent like a damp paper plate. We could see where the field light reflected in the sky and stopped short mid-air.

Always, we could hear trains.
    I remember thinking,
            I am from a place where I can always hear a train.
      then thinking
          Oh–

                         I am from a place.

My friend, Levi House, still writes to me from home. Each letter
Levi sends me photos of what he can see from his window. He lives
across from a dilapidated house that's right next to a funeral home.
He says he is also a House, who stares at them both for hours
on end.
    We will never move from a place that
               oh, we will never move from that *place.*

In Iceland, I write to Levi every day. I am trying to describe the
things I can see from my window. I write: *The sea is covered by fog. It's
like we came from nowhere.* The land in the distance — which is not
Greenland, but in my mind I secretly refer to as *Greenland* (my own
private Greenland) is gone.

I would like to know which piece of the plane makes *Glacier Girl*
more *Glacier Girl* than any other plane. It feels too late to know what
objects are important; what objects should be kept.
Everything with distance.
                      everything with
                distance.

Rabbit Rabbit Rabbit

We are sitting inside a morning. yellow. nice. We are drinking coffee. Joe just finished splitting logs and is telling me about his collection of body mysteries. Like, how all of his toes on his left foot have been sewn together since he was a baby. He and his mother can't remember why. Some things are just in the body, he says. The log pile cracks, shift. He tells me about a trick from growing up to get campfire smoke to blow the other way, say rabbit rabbit rabbit.

I must've not known about this trick because I am used to ash in my hair. I think I would like to try it with things completely unlike the things I'm sitting with now like: the motorcycles that rip under my bedroom window, the 28th of every month when my rent is due, or when I get the stench of stale whiskey in my nose while walking home alone at night — and I start thinking about the teapot. glazed Japanese maple red with a caned handle, left at my parents' house. My parents are trying to sell everything so they can live in an RV and are begging me to come and get the last of my stuff. I haven't been able to throw away the teapot or take it back in my carry-on each time I visit so I put it in my closet, further and further in. Every moment with the teapot is spent trying not to look at it.

rabbit rabbit rabbit

I have only ever brought one boyfriend home. The one who stamped his initials in the teapot before firing it. We didn't sleep in the same bed. He lay on the floor. Quiet and parallel because he was so afraid of all the guns in my father's house. The guns, I tried to explain, the metaphor is empty of firing. Pa is too soft for that — he used to take me into the forest and show me all the names of the trees. Every photo of my father is of his backside, gently sloped down to look at the bloom of foxfire. Goldenrods are his favorite because he is proud of where he is from. He loves Clark Gable the most. He used to wear his *Gone With the Wind* tie to the middle school on Fridays where he did not teach improper fractions but instead went around the class and asked each student what they thought he should eat for lunch (the answer would always turn out to be filet-o-fish) Pa's spine is crunching gravel. He points at trees from the porch when I visit. He is shorter now than when he was 14.

rabbit rabbitrabbit

Things that move slowly should be admired. The teapot is getting smaller. Things must make room for other things. Joe is standing up now. He places the toe of his boot near the fire to nudge a log back, revealing a rake of brushed ember. When I was little I used to think that if I stared at the inside of a fire long enough I would get over my fear of hell. What I saw instead was that hell looks lovely and can also be found in-between all sorts of things.

rab bitrabbit ra bbit

The teapot never held anything warmer than my hands. When my parents drove three days across the country to come get me from His house I sat in the back of the minivan with my box of sweaters, my dog, the teapot in my crossed lap as we careened through Montana. He asked me to take it. He wouldn't have had a complete dinner service anyway. some of the plates and cups he sculpted had gotten lost in the translation from arm. to head. to wall.

rr abbitrabbitrabbit

I'm afraid of writing about my dog because people may think he's boring. or worse. that most of my life revolves around an oily little animal who isn't that smart. My dog is showing up a lot lately. Like — now. He's in the back of the minivan with me, loosely rolling around. I am trying to hold onto both him and the teapot while my parents are in the front seats. My mother is shelling peanuts for Pa to eat. He keeps making this loud snorting sound as he hoovers up the peanuts from the heel of my mother's palm. She keeps batting him. laughing. and shelling more peanuts for him to eat. In this moment, I am completely miserable. I mistake love being behind me, receding.

rabbitr rr abbit   rabbit rab   b it

I've fallen asleep on buses before. I have the most vivid dreams where I smash that teapot over the guardrail. I dream of violence often enough that when I'm awake I'm afraid of how it'll change the look of my hands. I'm thinking of Mary Toft. How she said that she fell asleep while pregnant in a pasture and had a dream of a wanting so bad (of rabbits, braised with plums) that when she gave birth a few weeks later, she had a litter of pink warm bunnies. Somehow, she got the king of England to believe a woman's body could house rabbits.

rabbit

Joe & I are sitting quietly by one another. My dog lays behind his chair. We don't notice at first that the fire has gone out. White ash only. He goes on drinking coffee and I am amazed that things can be completely gone and they can also be here.

Cairn

Before we left up the mountain, he & I   shared this joke: if
we came across a bear, we only had to outrun each other. We
made each other laugh with our little horrors that summer.
Oh, when I say that this will be an ode to the work of
stacking stones, I mean to say that this is an ode to following
a path set by another. By then, I had only known the work of
walking. My calves unraveled like darned socks and my
toenails fell off one by one like baby teeth. That spring, I had
walked barefoot over the gravel of my landlady's driveway.
He said that I could use all the second skin I could get. That
work I'm talking about is trust. Like, when we came to that
river crossing, wide & deep from the year's snowmelt, we
saw a cairn on the bank near the berth of the violence. He
tightened the straps of his pack and said *After me, like this...*

     So I followed through his cut wake with the knife
edges of my feet. Stepping forward, suddenly to his waist —
he mistook what the water had meant. Later at camp, I shiv-
ered naked at his feet as he whipped the wet from my clothes
against the rocks. He said he was grabbing me away from
where I would've surely been swallowed whole. But when he
threw his arm back in the shape of a grasp, he hadn't looked
back to see where I was stepping next. Either way, I was
pulled under — my boots and socks peeled off like the river

recognized I was having a long day. He brought me to the surface by the crown of my head. On the other side, we lay on the bank still as the nearly dead. I pointed to another stack of stones across the river, yards further upstream by a quieter lull. There is a joke in that, sure. A clump of my hair was still tangled beneath his gold band, flashing as he beat my clothes dry. He paused, nodded down to my feet winking cod-white by the fire, *bet you're glad for that second skin now.* One day, I will return back to that cairn and pry up the violence, stone by stone. Leaving the wild as it was meant to be,   directionless.

These bees are still empty
filled only with the work of Grandpa Ed's
winter-gray June apples

        cloistered in the hilled orchard
        over by the empty school bus.

My family has flipped over
paper heavy combs to find want.

    Ed is alive again in that old bee suit
    now worn by a toddler and a half. Pa clutches the big empty hand.
               His own, uncovered.
    They float down the hill of fruit
    too hard and bitter even for the cows.

    Little cosmonaut on his voyage of honey
    he watches, still, as Pa opens up
    the clapboard of bees.
        Pa shows him a clump of workers
        humming a death knell in his flat, red palm.

We do not have the honey
that can be passed around the table
to fill each pore of white bread.

We have still been sweetened.

      Go on

        count the chickens

          the grass
          the fingers of that little deep sea diver

               he knows about honey.

July 17 / Tuolumne

We creep through
the meadows at Tuolumne,
my feet part through the grass.
Alpine pastures scrape against
God's knees. Birds break
in two then bend back
to swallow the mead
dripping from the sky.
Flies buzz above
the alkaline waters that push past us,
going west.
You've sunk a line
from the piece tied
to your trekking pole.
You reel back and tug.
A trout slips out of the water like a glove.
Its skin glints gold,
its empty orbs meet mine.
You try to slip
the hook from
its cheek. Your hands
haven't stopped tremoring
for two nights now

since that handle you drank
down in Yosemite.

You turn away from me.
With a suck pull
the hook slices through
trout's cheek, quick
and efficient
as a kiss.
You toss it back in the river.
I wish I'd looked for the secret prayer
slipped in between
the slick sun of the trout's scales.
I can't hold the pain
in the same sleeping way
as you.
In the meadow,
in this memory,
in Tuolumne,
I am the one
to gently place
the trout back in the water
feel it kick back
to life between my palms.

I let it swim away.

Driving Poem

Lately, I've been feeling like Jesus's sister.
Who knew that Jesus even had a sister?
In kindergarten, I learned "infant" was a special name for a baby.
I was so sad to have been born
just a baby. I should start asking for the things I want.
After I deliver the next bag of food to a customer I'll say,
"You realize you forgot to tip, right?"
My car smells like fried chicken.
This is what it's like to be the vehicle for someone else's desires.

I played volleyball for a season. My serves
never made it over the net.
I practiced the action of driving the ball while the team moved on
to other drills. Even now, I find myself mid-motion,
the heel of my wrist raised to strike
rubber from the air. Nothing comes down,
nothing gets over the net.

I thought my big Waiting would be done by now —
the rest of my life would be   *action*   *action*   *action.*
I want the same things that Eleanor Roosevelt did —
hot nasty speed
and also a little vegetable garden on the White House lawn.

I want everyone to know how fast and loose I live —
everyone except my mother. The other night I thought,
God it's been a tough summer.
Then realized,
it's been December.

Chekhov's Wristwatch

When I was 20 I flew for the first time
(for the first time in my life I mean).
The whole way I held up my nephew's fat bottom with the palm of my hand
while he pressed his melon against the window
and I kept trying to gently nudge his splayed fingers out of the way so I
could see too.

      Who did the Rockies look biggest to?
           Me,
                    who has been on the ground
                    (& for a while) who has looked up
                    at mountains from the ground after

knowing mountains
           or
                    him, whose whole bottom fits in a hand.

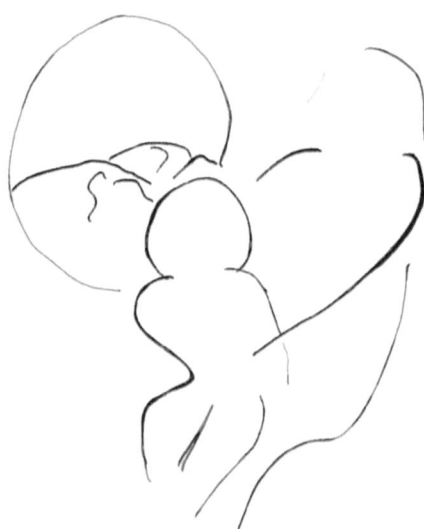

Notes

"Learning to Drive a Stick," "We are going up that hill," and "Carpenter Cemetery" were first published in *Appalachian Review*.

"July 17/Toulomne" and "Cairn" were first published in *Prairie Schooner*.

"These bees are still empty..." was first published in *Wake Forest Review*'s online edition.

"Horse Facts" was first published in *Tupelo Quarterly*.

"Basil" and "Chekhov's Wristwatch" were first published in *The Gravity of the Thing*.

"Swamp Molly" and "Driving Poem" were first published in *Pigeon Pages*.

Acknowledgments

Thank you Levi for helping me to make things.

Thank you Zachariah for always knowing what I mean.

Thank you to my family for the fodder.

About the Author

Makayla Danielle Gay hails from Southeastern Kentucky. She received her MFA from Sarah Lawrence College. Her essays, comics, and poems have appeared in the likes of *Adroit Journal*, *Action Spectacle*, and *Prairie Schooner*. She and her dog Mumford live in Seattle.